Make It Move

Leon Read

✳
SEA-TO-SEA
Mankato Collingwood London

Contents

Look for Tiger on the pages of this book. Sometimes he is hiding.

We move lots of things.

I move the
pen to draw.

Move Your Body

We make parts of our
bodies move.

Try moving these parts of your body.

arms

back

head

paw or hand

legs

Big and Small Moves

Some movements are big.

Some movements are small.

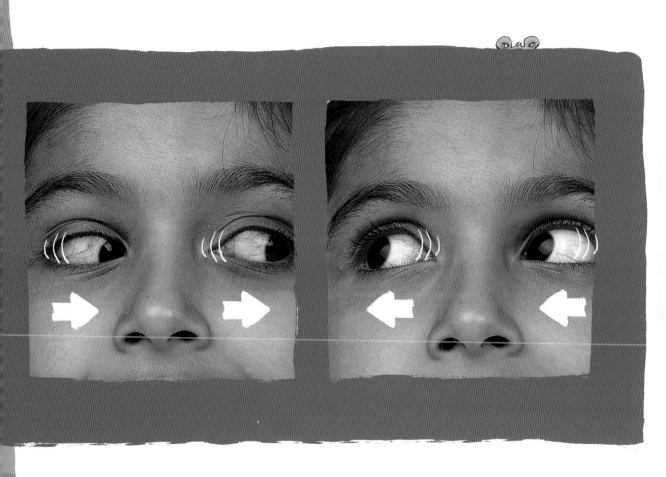

Can you wiggle your nose and your toes?

Pushing

We use parts of our bodies
to push things.

Tiger pushed this car.

push

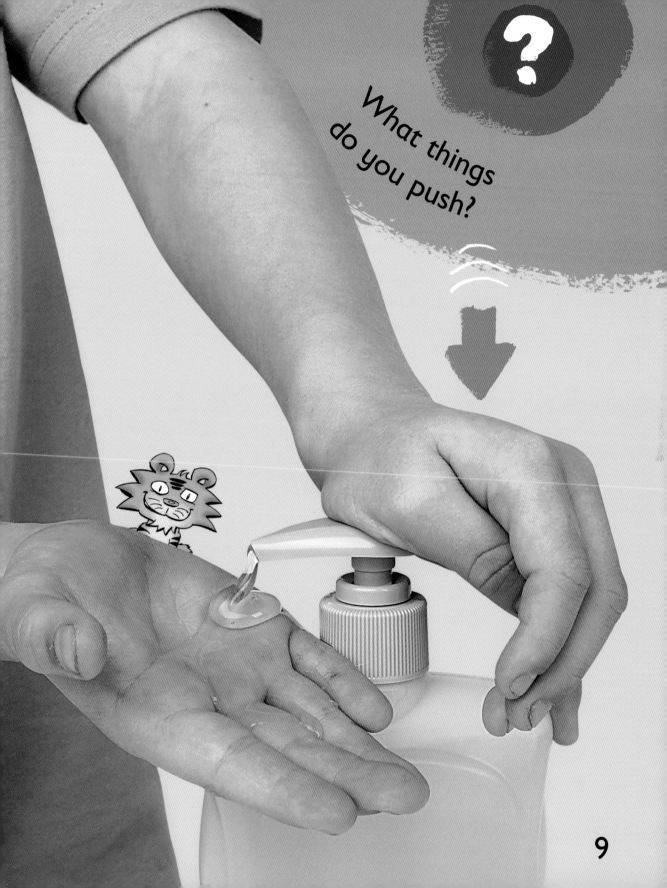

What things
do you push?

Pulling

We use parts of our bodies to pull things.

I'm pulling this suitcase.

pull

10

What things
do you pull?

Moving Games

We use things to make
other things move.

I push the ball with a paddle.

Moving Around

We can be moved with a push.

14

We can be moved
with a pull.

Stop!

I stop my bike
with the brakes.

I stopped this ball with my foot.

Why do we stop some things from moving?

17

Wind Power

Have you ever seen trees moving?

Or a kite flying?

The wind blows and moves things, too.

kite

sailboat

windmill

19

Look! No Hands

You can make things move without touching them.

I'm blowing this windmill.

21

Fast Wheels

Some things have
wheels to move.

fire engine

motorcycles

scooter

bicycles

Rani is looking for
things with wheels.
Make a list like hers.

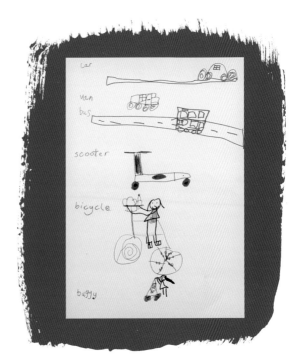

23

Word Picture Bank

Blow—pages 20, 21

Pull—pages 10, 11, 15

Push—pages 8, 9, 13, 1

Stop—pages 16, 17

Wheels—pages 22, 23

Windmill—page 19

This edition first published in 2011 by
Sea-to-Sea Publications
Distributed by Black Rabbit Books
P.O. Box 3263, Mankato, Minnesota 56002
Copyright © Sea-to-Sea Publications 2011
Printed in China, Dongguan
All rights reserved.

Library of Congress Cataloging-in-Publication Data
Read, Leon.
 Make it move / Leon Read.
   p. cm. -- (Tiger talk. Get into science)
 Summary: "Provides young readers with an introduction to health and
fitness and describes basic body movements and actions"--Provided by
publisher.
 ISBN 978-1-59771-251-4 (lib. bd.)
1. Human locomotion--Juvenile literature. 2. Human mechanics--Juvenile
literature. I. Title.
 QP301.R426 2011
 612.7'6--dc22
                                        2009053789

9 8 7 6 5 4 3 2

Published by arrangement with the Watts Publishing Group Ltd, London.

Series editor: Adrian Cole
Photographer: Andy Crawford (unless otherwise credited)
Design: Sphere Design Associates
Art director: Jonathan Hair
Consultants: Prue Goodwin and Karina Law

Acknowledgments:
The Publisher would like to thank Norrie Carr model agency. "Tiger" puppet used
with kind permission from Ravensden PLC (www.ravensden.co.uk). Tiger Talk logo
drawn by Kevin Hopgood. Picture Credits: Keith Brofsky/Brand X/Corbis (14).
Guillermo Hung/DK Stock/Getty Images (15).

Every attempt has been made to clear copyright.
Should there be any inadvertent omission, please
apply to the publisher for rectification.

March 2010
RD/6000006414/002

There are 15 Tigers, including me, in this bo
Did you find all of us?